ART TREASURES OF ASIA
GENERAL EDITOR: JANE GASTON MAHLER

TURKISH MINIATURE PAINTING

Edited with Introduction and Notes, by

Emel Esin

CHARLES E. TUTTLE COMPANY
RUTLAND, VERMONT & TOKYO, JAPAN

Contents

INTRODUCTION   3

PLATE 1: Adam and Eve   8

PLATE 2: The Beast of the Earth   10

PLATE 3: Ezekiel Raising the Dead   12

PLATE 4: The Nativity of Muhammed   14

PLATE 5: Muhammed on Mount Hira   16

PLATE 6: Muhammed Praying with Khadija and Ali   18

PLATE 7: The Death of Muhammed   20

PLATE 8: The Enthronement of Selim II   22

PLATE 9: The Turkish Army Departing for the Caucasian Campaign, April 1578   24

PLATE 10: Episode from the Festivities at Istanbul in September 1720   26

PLATE 11: Nocturnal Party on the Sea of Marmora   28

PLATE 12: A Turkish Lady of the 18th Century   30

NOTES   32

SELECTED BIBLIOGRAPHY   32

ILLUSTRATIONS   33

Introduction

by Emel Esin

LIGHT has recently been shed on Turkish miniature painting through two new sources. The rich collections of the Ottoman sultans have become accessible and have provided a wealth of new material, and the accumulated results of archeological research during the past fifty years have revealed new elements of knowledge concerning the antecedents of Turkish art. Therefore it is now possible to draw a tentative sketch of the origins and development of Turkish miniature painting.

Some three thousand years ago, in the region extending over the northern and central parts of Asia, from the outskirts of eastern Europe to the borders of China, there lived various ethnic stocks who, according to historical, anthropological, linguistic, and cultural evidence, were among the ancestors of the Turks. Turkish annals have preserved the memory of the legendary kings and their peoples who lived in the "land of Turan" under tents, wore golden crowns, rode speedy horses, and used animal figures as heraldic emblems. Their cattle-branding seals are reproduced in Turkish documents.

These nomadic peoples had, from the oldest times, developed artistic traditions whose original character is being disclosed by archeological discoveries. From mounds and ice-bound tombs there have emerged examples of metalwork, sculpture, carpets, textiles, and other creations that, although scattered over wide areas in northern and central Asia and eastern Europe, present a remarkable unity in concept and design. In his figural works, the nomad artist has often described the early inhabitants of the vast steppes of Eurasia. They appear to be of two main ethnic types, specimens of which can be seen on a felt-appliqué tent cover from the 4th century B.C. and in a sculptured head from about the 3rd century A.D. The former represents a hook-nosed Altaic Scythian; the latter, a Hunnic type. (See Illustrations 1 and 2. All text illustrations are shown on pages 33–34.) The Hun and the Altaic Scythian of two to three thousand years ago were dressed in costumes designed for riding: tight-fitting tunics, jackets, trousers which become narrow or are gathered at the ankle, boots. and crown-shaped headgear or fur bonnets.[1]

The nomad artist, living in close communion with nature, has also depicted the swift movements of the animals of his abode: both those that are wild, such as the migrating bird, the reindeer, the boar, and the tiger, and those tamed by him, such as the horse and cattle. The sense of the supernatural, inherent in a follower of animistic beliefs, is expressed in fabulous creatures displaying an unnatural combination of body parts—for instance, human-headed and winged quadrupeds (Ill. 1). Abstract designs and plant patterns are also often represented.[2]

Ancient nomadic art has continued to live tenaciously throughout the centuries in its almost unchanged primitive form, flourishing until our day mainly in the popular arts of Central Asia and Turkey (Ill. 3). The spontaneous, dynamic, and expressive works of ancient nomadic art seem in some instances to have provided patterns for the development of later Central Asian, Chinese, and Iranian designs. It is necessary to look first to Central Asia for the origins of Turkish art.

According to legend, when Feridun, "one of the oldest kings of the world," divided his realm between his two sons Ir and Tur, Ir settled in Iran, and Tur in Turan, in the north. Their descendants are said to be the Iranians and the Turks.

Central Asia, a region included in the legendary land of Turan, is among the oldest centers of civilization in the world. The settlement at Anau in Turkmenistan, east of the Caspian Sea, is thought by archeologists to be some six thousand years old. Zarathustra (Zoroaster), according to tradition, was born in the town of Balkh in Bactria in the 6th or 7th century B.C. The fabulous city of the Turanian king Alp Ertonga, called Afrasiyab by the Iranians, is also reported to have been located in Central Asia.

In the first centuries of the Christian era, artistic production in Central Asia, particularly in painting, reached a high degree of achievement. It is this Central Asian art that is the immediate predecessor of Turkish painting. In the words of a commentator on one of the 16th-century manuscripts in the Topkapu Museum in Istanbul: "Mani (founder of the Manicheist faith) claimed prophethood and made his prophet's claim acceptable in the eyes of men through the miracle of painting. . . . Thereafter, he went in the direction of Khatay and there produced wonderful works of art."

This tradition, repeated in all Islamic and Turkish chronicles as well as in Turkish poetry, where the

3

"images of Khotan" are often mentioned, has been confirmed through archeological excavations. Before Mani founded his religion in the 3rd century A.D., Buddhism had crossed the borders of India into Central Asia and had acquired in that region pictorial and plastic forms that were to endure in Buddhist art. Buddhist and Manichean temples were built, as well as monasteries for Buddhist monks and for the priests of the local Magian religion of Zarathustra. Archeologists working in Central Asia have unearthed literally thousands of grottos and temples in which were found mural paintings, clay sculpture, illustrated manuscripts, and inscriptions in several languages, dating from the first centuries after Christ. Among the inscriptions were many Turkish ones written in a specifically Turkish alphabet. These enable us to fix at about the 6th century the origins of Turkish painting. Works of art of the first centuries of the Christian era found in Central Asian settlements often possess the same expressive, dynamic quality observed in ancient nomadic art.

At sites ranging from Samarkand and Bukhara to Kansu in present-day China, a vast and heterogeneous world had been represented in which figured a complete hierarchy of beings: celestial creatures, men, animals, and demons. Among the human figures represented in this art, the old Pazyryk Scythian and Hunnic ethnic types, wearing costumes similar to those of the ancient nomads, are predominant, although a European type is shown as well. One also sees heavenly beings with luminous or flaming halos, round-faced sun or moon gods, monks, warriors, and ladies sometimes holding lotus offerings reminiscent of old Eurasian floral themes. These figures may be riding horseback, engaging in Buddhist meditation, performing in concerts, or feasting with cup in hand while sitting in the cross-legged fashion that was later to be called the "Turkish way of sitting" (Ill. 4).

The Buddha figures, in traditional Indian poses, are shown with features characteristic of Central Asian ethnic types. The animals of the old nomadic art reappear, having undergone slight variations. Composite human and animal creatures are also represented, together with some purely human ones in fantastic shapes having, for instance, a multiplication of limbs, as in Hindu style or as in astral figures of the Sabeans and the Mongolians. At Kyzyl in Turkestan, in the 7th century, hell was represented with monstrous inhabitants. Symbolic meanings connected with the then reigning schools of thought have been attributed to these fabulous creatures, about which Buddhist and Manichean texts, as well as Islamic literature of the Seljuk period from the 11th through the 13th century provide information.

Exchanges of influence with Indian, Chinese, Sassanid Iranian, and Hellenistic arts are discernible in these works. The patterns of Central Asian art were destined to spread far into the world: to the Buddhist countries, like China in the Northern Wei period; to Europe, probably through migrating groups of Manicheans; and, after Islam, to the entire Near East and India.

The repercussions on art of the adoption of Islam in Central Asia after the 7th century were far-reaching. Most of the early painting and sculpture of the region had been created in the service of the various pre-Islamic religions. After the 7th century the peoples of the region, particularly those of the western areas of Central Asia, began to abandon this multitude of gods n favor of the Islamic concept, which defines God as above human imagination and pictorial expression. Therefore, in Islamic regions of Turkestan, the painting of religious images ceased. Religious art was limited to calligraphy in Koranic texts, where Arabic characters replaced the old Uigur Turkish script and illumination consisted of decorative designs in the local tradition, such as the old *tamga* or seal patterns. Abstract patterns were developed, and symbolic meanings were attributed to some of them.

Painting held its ground in the worldly domain, although figural representations were largely confined to book illustration. Among these early specimens of Islamic art, some designs and techniques characteristic of Turkestan (Khirbet-ul-Mafjar, Samarra, etc.) confirm the reports of Oriental chroniclers that Turkestani artists were working in the Near East.

While an Islamic Turkestani art was evolving in Central Asia after the 7th century, in the nearby lands of the Uigur Turks Buddhist and Manicheist figural art continued to develop, as may be seen in the frescoes and manuscripts found in Khocho and Tun-huang. In Moslem eyes these non-Islamic regions of Turkestan were part of China's sphere of influence. The Tunguz Khatay that ruled North China had invaded Turkestan in the 11th century. Thereafter the name "Khatay" was used in Oriental manuscripts to designate both areas. Some of these manuscripts in the libraries of Istanbul contain accounts of 13th- and 15th-century travels to "Khatay, the land of the Kaan" (Kaan or Khan being the title of Turkish and Mongol rulers). There are also many miniatures and drawings, some with Turkish inscriptions in Uigur characters, attributed to the "masters of Khatay." These are very similar in style to the paintings and sculpture of the last phase of the work represented in Khocho and Tun-huang. Non-Islamic subjects and adaptations of Buddhist motifs to Islamic themes continue to be used in Turkish art of later periods. In the Topkapu Museum (Miscellanies Nos. H. 2152–61) there are miniatures that are considered to be very old and that seem to be related to Buddhist or Manicheist iconology.

Among numerous more recent works, those of Mehmed Siyah Kalem may be noted. In the Miscellanies, as elsewhere, the admiration of the Islamic painters for the artists of "Khatay and Khotan" is expressed. The terms "moon-faced Khotan image" and *bud,* or "idol," were used to describe a beautiful person. An 18th-century poem in Turkish by Sheyh Galib (Hüsn ve Ashk) places the "Castle of Images," symbol of worldly temptations, in a land bordering on China.

The development of Turkish miniature painting entered a new phase after the 11th century, following the migration and establishment of some of the Turkish peoples in Turkey. It was after the 10th century that these bands had begun to penetrate the Near East, bringing with them the artistic traditions of the ancient Eurasian nomads and of Turkestan. The Seljuk Turks founded a state extending from Turkestan through Iran, Mesopotamia, and Anatolia. In Baghdad in the 12th century they established the first Islamic school of miniature painting, and it seems probable that there were Uigur Turks among the artists.[3] One group of Turks had moved into Anatolia in the 11th century. Later waves came in from Central Asia, the Volga regions, Crimea, and the Balkans at the time of the Mongol invasion in the 13th century. It was then that the Ottoman branch arrived. Related groups, driven by the armies of Genghis Khan, settled in Khorassan, Azerbaijan, and other areas near the Caspian Sea. These regions, then being predominantly Turkicized, formed a bridge between the old homelands and the new.

The Mongols were indebted to the Uigur Turks for the language and the alphabet that they officially adopted in the western part of their realm. An original Tabriz manuscript of the Mongol period (Vakifnameyi Rashiduddin) lists the names of twenty Turkish painters, calligraphers, architects, and other craftsmen employed by the Mongol rulers of Azerbaijan.[4] In the reign of Hulagu Khan, Buddhist temples in the same province were adorned with murals.[5] At Afyon Kara Hisar, in Turkey, a Buddha image was excavated some twenty years ago.

The old artistic traditions of the nomadic tribes and of pre-Islamic Central Asia influenced and enriched this new development of miniature painting. In color, composition, and even in detail we can note resemblances. The same rules concerning hierarchical scale, symbolic gesture, pose, colors, and attributes which govern the universe concept of pre-Islamic Turkestani painting have been partially preserved in the later miniatures. For example, a central figure, usually representing a ruler beneath an *otag* (ruler's tent), is shown seated in a regal pose, generally with legs crossed (Ill. 4 and 5) and surrounded by symmetrical groups of secondary figures who kneel or stand with hands clasped. This formal plan reflects the tribal etiquette of Central Asia. Persons of Hunnic, Altaic Scythian, and West Turkish[6] ethnic types are represented.

When the painters of Turkestan migrated to the Is-lamic countries, they had the task of representing many new figures such as angels, prophets, mystics, holy warriors, Islamic ladies, kings, and finally the genii of the Near East. It was natural to give these new subjects the shapes of analogous figures in the old Turkestani iconology. In this way, hosts of pre-Islamic Turkestani creatures entered into Islamic miniature painting. These included crowned personages like those seen in the paintings at Panj-Kent (Ill. 6), holy men riding tigers or elephants as in Tun-huang art, hermits sitting in Turkish fashion among animals, kings enthroned amidst their courts, composite beasts (Ill. 1), astral figures and other fabulous beings with composite or multiple limbs, many-headed angels like the Avalokitesvara from Toyok,[7] infernal monsters, and numerous other subjects. Costume elements from the nomadic period have also survived down to our day in the national dress of the Mongols; of the Kazak, Uzbek, and Kirgiz Turks in Central Asia; and of the Turkmen in Turkmenistan and Turkey. These can be seen in the tunics, jackets, trousers narrowing down or gathered at the ankles, embroidered or plain boots, crown-shaped or brimmed felt bonnets, fur-lined hats, cylindrical or conical headdresses, and helmets which may be pointed or surmounted by a pin and ball (Ill. 7). It is to be noted that these costumes, together with Hunnic features, are reserved by Turkish painters for all who originate from the land of Turan, starting with the legendary king Feridun and coming down to the 15th-century Turkmen king Uzun Hasan. On the other hand, the Turks of Turkey are usually made to wear the turban associated with Islam.

Some gestures characteristic of old Turkestani painting have also remained. In a 15th-century miniature, for example, Sultan Mehmed II is shown holding a flower in much the same way as did Uigur princes and ladies in the Buddhist murals and votive banners of the 8th century. Similarly, we can find stylized floral borders of the type used as early as 400 B.C. as an adjunct to the goddess and devotee on an embroidered felt from Pazyryk. Musical instruments remain almost unchanged over the centuries, from the 2nd-century Tirmiz frieze in Turkestan to the 18th-century Ottoman concert scenes. The same parallels may be observed in the use of the *tamga, otag,* cups, floral motifs, landscape elements, and other conventions.

Until further study is made of Seljuk painting on wood and of the figural ceramics of Anatolia, and these are compared with the rich collections of early illustrated manuscripts of Istanbul and other Turkish cities, any attempt to describe the evolution of Turkish miniature painting must be confined to an enumeration of separate facts. Among these we may note that Turkish painters, like men of other professions, were led by a head or master. The head painter was called *nakkashbashi.* The patron saint of painters is said to be Ali, the fourth caliph of Islam. The artists worked together in groups of masters and pupils, forming schools under the protection of a patron or independently. The masters accepted commissions to illustrate texts which they illuminated, sometimes making several copies, either alone or with the aid of their pupils. These illustrated texts fall into the following general categories:

a) The lives of the prophets and the saints and works of religious edification. Although figural elements exist in some of these, as a rule the holy personages are shown veiled (Plates IV, V, and VI). They may also be suggested by such symbols as swords or flames. Many religious paintings are connected with the Bektashi order of dervishes who had a special veneration for the patron saint Ali.

b) Works relating to the lives of legendary Turanian kings, for instance Afrasiyab, to whom every Turkish ruler has in some way tried to link himself; the lives of conquerors or other famous men of Central Asia, such as Genghis Khan or Tamerlane; accounts of campaigns of the Ottoman Turks; and biographies of sultans, men of letters, and other eminent persons.

c) Poetical works in Turkish or in Arabic and Persian, which were the international scholarly languages of the Islamic world.

d) Treatises on such sciences as geography (maps and travel books), astronomy, botany, medicine, or the "science of ciphers," a field associated with mysticism.

e) Books on such sports as falconry, horsemanship, archery, and sailing.

Out of commendable humility, many Turkish painters refrained from signing their work. From chronicles and archives, Turkish scholars have gathered information on the identity of some of these painters. This can be summarized by periods as follows:

Konya period (12th and 13th centuries): In this initial phase, in Turkey's first capital, Konya, the walls of the Meram kiosks were decorated by a painter called Bedreddin Yavash (the Slow). Another painter, Aynuddevle, painted portraits of the poet Jelaluddin Rumi and others. There are paintings in a private collection in Konya, in the Aya Sofya Library (Nos. 3702 and 3704), and in the Topkapu Museum of Istanbul (No. H. 841) which seem to be of the Konya Seljuk period. These miniatures show figures resembling those seen in ceramics and sculptures of the same time in Konya and elsewhere in Anatolia.

Bursa and Edirne periods (14th and 15th centuries): A certain "Ali the Painter" is said to have decorated the Green Mosque in Bursa, second capital of Turkey, in the 14th century. Another Ali was taken to Samarkand after the invasion of Anatolia by Tamerlane but returned later to Turkey. According to old payrolls, the imperial palace of Edirne, third Turkish capital, was decorated by mural painters.

Istanbul period (15th to 18th centuries): In the 15th century a portrait of Mehmed II, now in the Topkapu Museum, was painted by the Turkish painter Sinan Bey. Bayezid II, to whose interest we owe the classification of many illustrated manuscripts in the Istanbul libraries (as witnessed by his seal), had a painter called Baba Mustafa Nakkash (Father Mustafa the Painter) who painted mural and miniature works. Under Selim I, Nakkash Tajeddin and Hasan are mentioned. At this time the walls of a kiosk at the Topkapu Palace were decorated with paintings. In the 16th century, at the court of Süleyman the Magnificent, we find academies of painting where local and foreign artists worked. The portraits of the famous Admiral Hayreddin Pasha and others, now in the Topkapu Museum, were done by the Turkish painter Nigari.

After the 16th century, we meet many renowned painters, including Osman, Kalender, Nakshi, Hasan Pasha, Said, Ibrahim, Mimi Celebi of Galata, Hayali, Rahmi, and Zati. Some of the works of Osman at the Topkapu Museum are the *Hünername* (Nos. H. 1523 and H. 1524), the *Surname* (No. H. 1344), and the *Kiyafeti Insaniye fi Shemaili Osmaniye* (Nos. H. 1562 and H. 1563). Kalender painted a *falname* (book of fortunetelling) for Sultan Ahmed I which is at the Topkapu Museum. Nakshi illustrated several anthologies with portraits of celebrated philosophers, mystics, and poets. The great painter of the 18th century is Levni, some of whose works are the *Surname-i Vehbi* (No. A. III. 3594) and several framed miniatures in the Topkapu Museum. Abdullah Buhari, who painted some miniatures now in the Topkapu Museum, may have been, according to his name, a Central Asian from Bukhara.

Turkish miniature painting led an independent existence conditioned by Turkish life and ways of expression. The Mongol-period schools of painting in Azerbaijan and the later schools of Central Asia, such as those of Samarkand and Herat, as well as the Safavid schools of Iran and the Mughal school of India, were, like Turkish miniature painting, the separately flowering offshoots of the same old Central Asian tree. Exchanges were maintained between Turkish painters and painters of these kindred schools.

The *Hünername* tells of a visit to Istanbul by a group "from the land of Turan" which results in the painting of a portrait of Mehmed II in the 15th century. In connection with this visit, Ali Kushci, a pupil of the Timurid astronomer-prince of Samarkand, Ulug Bey, is mentioned. This information points to the possibility that the visiting painters came from a Central Asian miniature center like Samarkand or Herat. Istanbul libraries contain many miniatures of these two schools, as well as portrait drawings of Timur and his descendants arranged in traditional Central Asian compositions with Uigur inscriptions. On the whole, we may recognize themes and figures inspired by the later Central Asian schools of Samarkand and Herat perhaps less in Turkish miniature painting than in Safavid Iranian and Mughal Indian miniatures. The Turkish painter of the Ahmed I Miscellany Collection No. H. 408 in the Topkapu Museum says, however, that he emulates not only the masters of Turkey but also those of Khatay (Central Asia), Sultaniye (Mongol, 14th century), and Samarkand (15th to 16th century). A visit of the 16th-century Azerbaijan painter Shah Kuli to Istanbul is illustrated in a Turkish miniature. An inscription in a Topkapu Museum manuscript (No. H. 2154) refers to the presence at the Safavid court of a Shah Kuli Rumi, whose surname Rumi indicates that he was a Turkish Anatolian.

In keeping with other aspects of Turkish art, miniature painting has a vigorous personality and an unconventional approach despite certain traditional rules of composition and the symbolism attributed to colors. The Turk loves to depict, sometimes humorously, bodies in movement and is at his best when he is portraying crowds or genre scenes. He does not idealize his subject, preferring to present it in the guise of everyday life as observed by the artist. The drawing style of the Turkish painter is an expressionistic one using few lines and epitomizing the source of the artist's inspiration. A minutely detailed execution is rarely seen in Turkish works, which are often of a larger size than "miniature" would imply. This may be explained by the fact that, in Turkestan, mural painting preceded miniatures.

Using pigment mixed with white of egg, the Turk covers surfaces with colors whose brilliance "would put the sun to shame." Together with patches of contrasting color, he often uses subtly graduated nuances of the same shade. In religious painting, deep emotion is expressed through austere simplicity. By such characteristics, Turkish miniature painting differentiates itself from the lyrical graces of the Persian miniatures and the detailed perfection of Mughal Indian painting and may be said to emerge as a direct descendant of the ancient nomadic and pre-Islamic Turkestani arts.

In the present work, only miniatures from the late 16th to the 18th century are shown. This is the result of a desire to convey the atmosphere of an epoch which, having lost nothing of the traditional aspect of Turkish miniature painting, left the richest legacy of works in the fields of religious and secular art.

Byzantine painting, as well as European painting, even at the time of the visit of Gentile Bellini to Istanbul around 1477, had failed to leave an imprint on Turkish art. Toward the end of the 18th century, European painting penetrated Turkey, together with the whole of the European way of life. Miniature painting now began to be supplanted by oil painting. An important factor in this change was the adaptation of the printing press to Arabic characters, achieved in Istanbul in 1727 by Ibrahim Müteferrika, the founder of Islamic typography. Thereafter, the writing and illustrating of manuscripts gradually ceased. Nevertheless, miniature painting in the Turkish manner is still taught at the Academy of Fine Arts in Istanbul, as well as in private schools.

PLATE ONE

Adam and Eve

From a falname (book of fortunetelling) written in Turkish for Sultan Ahmed I and illustrated by the painter Kalender with thirty-six miniatures on paper illuminated with flower designs. 17th century. 47.5 ×34.5 cm. Courtesy of the Topkapu Museum (H. 1703), Istanbul.

THE ARTIST has chosen the dramatic moment of the expulsion of Adam and Eve from paradise. Both figures are large enough to cover the foreground. They are placed slightly to the left side, as if about to leave the Garden of Eden. Adam and Eve are hand in hand, their contrition shown in their facial expressions. Eve still holds in one hand the forbidden fruit, which in Near Eastern concept is a sheaf of wheat. Her head and Adam's are surrounded by flaming halos, prototypes of which are seen in pre-Islamic Uigur miniatures or in sculptures like those of Tun-huang (Ill. 8).

Flowers are blooming in the Garden of Eden in stylized patterns reminiscent of the Turkestani Buddhist lotus. A naturalistic serpent holds some leaves in its mouth, thus indicating that Adam and Eve have just been taught to wear vine or fig leaves. A delicate structure with an arcade of violet marble supported by fragile red columns forms the background. Through the arcade is seen the blue-green color associated in Islam with the celestial gardens. A fine web of decoration in hexagonal and other geometric patterns covers the heavenly edifice, giving it an elusive appearance. These patterns resemble those seen in the tiles of 14th- and 15th-century mosques at Bursa, Turkey's second capital.

An angel stands at the side gate of paradise, counterbalancing the movement in the figures of Adam and Eve and, at the same time, giving a sense of depth through its smaller size. The dress of the angel is red, a color symbolic of the burning love between God and man that will eventually consume the evil in mankind. The wings show some feathers in blue, the color of purity. The tunic, in a style usual in 17th-century Turkey, is girdled with a belt which is described in the literature of the Turkish order of Bektashi dervishes (connected through the Yesevi dervishes with Central Asia) as the *tekvaa* or belt of "reticence from evil." The angelic girdles in Turkish paintings closely resemble the girdles of pre-Islamic holy figures in Turkestan. The Turkish angels wear closed crowns, a prototype of which is seen in a 7th-century painting at Panj-Kent (Ill. 6). The nomad goddess of Pazyryk also wore, 2,400 years ago, a crown-shaped headgear (Ill. 9). The crowns may be explained by the fact that in Central Asian cosmogony the temporal world is ruled by heroes and the spiritual world by celestial beings and holy men. The 9th-century Uigur king Idikut (Holy Majesty) combined temporal and spiritual powers, and the title Spiritual Ruler was extended to Moslem Turkish holy men.

Together with the angel, a peacock is chasing Adam and Eve from heaven. The 13th-century poet of Central Asian origin, Jelaluddin Rumi, tells us that this bird personifies man's desire for worldly life *(hirs)*.

8

The Beast of the Earth

From a falname *(book of fortunetelling) written in Turkish for Sultan Ahmed I and illustrated by the painter Kalender with thirty-six miniatures on paper illuminated with flower designs. 17th century. 47.5 ×34.5 cm. Courtesy of the Topkapu Museum (H. 1703), Istanbul.*

THE BEAST of the Earth is an allegory of the material world in the shape of a creature with composite limbs. This large figure, which may hardly be called a miniature painting, is pictorially in the tradition of ancient Central Asia, although it bears a Koranic and apocalyptic name. The *falname* figure is associated with one of the oldest fabulous creatures of Central Asia: the one represented in Pazyryk in the Altai Mountains, 2,400 years ago, over a nomad's tent in felt-appliqué technique (Ill. 1). The Beast of the Earth may also be compared to the 7th-century Kyzyl Garuda of Turkestan and to many other pre-Islamic Central Asian figures. It is, moreover, related to some popular representations of Seljuk and Ottoman genii.

How did the 2,400-year-old Central Asian figure come to acquire a Koranic and apocalyptic name and, furthermore, to symbolize the material world? The connections seem to have been established in two phases. When, after the 11th century, some of the Turkish peoples of Central Asia migrated to the Near East, they brought with them artists who were now called upon to represent the various historical and fabulous characters of the Near Eastern lands. These artists must have sought in their own iconology shapes that might be considered equivalents. As we have noted in the Introduction, there are many examples of this process. The genii of Islamic miniatures may also be affiliated with the composite animal shapes of Central Asia. A 7th-century Manichean Turkish miniature, representing a seated central figure surrounded by celestial creatures and elephant- or dog-headed fabulous animals, may well be considered a prototype of many Islamic miniatures showing Solomon amidst his court composed of angels, men, and animal-shaped genii. The creature whom the Koran calls "worse than the beast" and who seems to have here acquired the external shape of a Central Asian monster is, in Islamic tradition, interpreted as an image of the ultimate degradation to which mankind, devoid of spiritual force, may fall. It is therefore identified with attachment to the material world.

In this illustration, the beast grows from the earth, together with flowers, at the foot of a mauve hill. Although he is equipped with a pair of wings, the bracelets around his ankles and wrists chain him to the earth. In the allegoric images of the Koran, if unholy creatures want to raise themselves to higher spheres of perception, they are chased with flames. These we see coming down in stylized form from the upper border of the miniature.

The mythical monster has, like the Central Asian figure, a pair of wings, a male human head, a pair of horns, a decorative fan-shaped tail in red, and the arms and legs of a tiger, an animal symbolizing anger. The Beast of the Earth presents, moreover, ome peculiarities. His canine teeth are overdeveloped. He holds in his hands the implements of an ancient game, the ring and the arrow. He wears earrings, and around his neck is a golden collar decorated with animal heads and a bell with which, in Near Eastern tradition, he is said to make a deafening noise. Like the 7th-century Turkestani Garuda, he has the torso of a bird, in this instance a peacock, symbol of worldly desires.

Ezekiel Raising the Dead

From the Zübdet-üt-Tevarih *(Epitome of Historical Works), written in Turkish for Sultan Murad III in 1583 and containing thirty-eight miniatures 65 × 42 cm each. 16th century. 42 × 42 cm (part of a page). Courtesy of the Türk-Islam Eserleri Museum (Museum of Turkish-Islamic Art) (MS No. 1973), Istanbul.*

THE MINIATURES of the *Zübdet-üt-Tevarih* display for the most part a stately beauty and show such brilliant colors as red, orange, blue, and mauve. In true Turkish tradition, the colors are not only arranged in contrasting surfaces but also present different variations of the same hues.

Ezekiel stands in a desolate landscape done in the 7th-to-8th-century pre-Islamic Turkestani style (Ill. 10). The hills rise like flames in mauve-rose opalescent colors, typical of 16th-to-17th-century Turkish work, against a golden sky. (Gold is the "surrealist" element in the Turkish miniature, often indicating that an unnatural event is taking place.) The dead are seen emerging from open tombs in the sands of the desert. Bones and skulls are scattered on the ground. Ezekiel, who because of his small size seems lost in the desert, has a flaming golden halo. He is dressed in Turkish clerical garb and wears a turban. The turban, although seen in Central Asian sculpture as early as the 5th century—for example, in the stucco heads at Hadda in Afghanistan—is associated with Islam, Muhammed having worn a headband on some occasions.

The painter represents Ezekiel as a Moslem because the Moslems consider monotheist believers of all faiths and times as their own. The raising of the dead by the prophets is interpreted in Islamic mysticism as the spiritual reawakening of the soul.

In the Topkapu Museum in Istanbul there is a "Book of Genealogies," the *Silsilename,* written by the judge Lokman Ashuri for the grand vizier Siyavush Pasha in the same period as the *Zübdet-üt-Tevarih* and presenting many points of similarity with it in subject, illustrations, and size. The Chester Beatty Collection of Dublin also possesses a book, smaller in size, called *Zübdet-üt-Tevarih.*[8]

The Istanbul *Zübdet-üt-Tevarih* and the *Silsilename* begin with the same illuminated Koranic inscription: "Blessed is He who created the heavens and the earth and made darkness and light." In the *Silsilename* the author says: "I, the weakest of the servants of God, the humblest of the soldiers of God, wanted to describe the mighty creation and the certitude of the reign and presence of the Creator. May He be glorified."

The object of all three of these books was to summarize the various notions on religion, astronomy, history, and geography that were of importance to a Turk of the 16th century. The manuscripts include some traditional opinions; popular ideas on the creation of the universe; the stories of Adam and Eve and of Noah; episodes dealing with the origins of the Turks; the lives of the Biblical prophets, Christ, Muhammed, and the first caliphs and imams; genealogies of ruling families in Turkestan and the Near East; and the history of the Seljuk, Karaman, and Ottoman dynasties in Turkey.

The miniatures in the Chester Beatty *Zübdet-üt-Tevarih* are said to be by a painter called Sun'i. The names of the illustrators of the two Istanbul manuscripts are unknown. There is a resemblance in the composition of the miniatures in all three works.

The Nativity of Muhammed

From the three-volume manuscript, Siyer-un-Nebi *(Progress of the Prophet): a copy: executed in 1594 by Ahmet Nur b. Mustafa for Murad III, of an earlier manuscript dated 1368, whose author was Mustafa b. Yusuf b. Omer Erzeni Dariri. One of 125 miniatures. 16th century. 15×14.5 cm. Courtesy of the Topkapu Museum (H. 1221–23), Istanbul.*

THE MINIATURES of the *Siyer-un-Nebi* are among the best examples of Turkish religious art.[9] They are nobly drawn, luminous in color, strong in composition, and deep in religious feeling.

In this example we see, in a room that might be a rural *mescid* or chapel, the infant Muhammed surrounded by a symmetrical group composed of his mother Amine and three angels. The floor of the room is covered with straw mats, and the walls are decorated in Turkish style with niches and with tiles of the Bursa period in geometric patterns. The two inscriptions on the wall are connected with the event of the Nativity. The *mihrab* (prayer niche) and the arcades present an ogival form of arch traditional in Turkish architecture since its 7th-century origin in Turkestan. Within the *mihrab* burns the lamp or *misbah* mentioned in the Koran and interpreted by the poet Jelaluddin Rumi as a representation of the human soul.

The face of the child Muhamed is veiled, as are the faces of other holy figures in Turkish miniatures, both out of reverence and out of reluctance to portray features that would fail to achieve true resemblance. The newborn infant, clad in pink, is already making the symbolic gesture of purification by performing the ritual ablutions. Three angels with Hunnic features are assisting in this act, presenting to him in Turkish fashion the basin, the ewer, and the towel. The angels wear crowns of Central Asian shape and Turkish robes in green, blue, and red: colors respectively symbolizing resurrection, purity, and divine love. The child is surrounded by the "light of Muhammed," a flaming golden halo that blazes upward. This light is interpreted by Erzeni and other Turkish mystics as representing the love of virtue and justice, inspired first in Adam, accepted by him as a trust, and inherited by generation after generation of just men and pure women among his descendants.

The mother of Muhammed, also veiled, appears in a *ferace* or mantle in the fashion of a lady of Istanbul. We can guess that under the veil she is wearing a *hotoz* or *tepelik*, a headdress used since pre-Islamic days and displayed in Turkestani sculpture of the 7th and 8th centuries. With the adoption of Islam, Turkish women covered their headdresses with the Moslem veil, emblem of modesty. The veiled figure of the kneeling woman, her hands raised in a gesture of surprise at the wonders of the night of Nativity, suggests the lines of the 14th-century "Poem of Nativity" (Mevlid) by Süleyman Celebi, which is still often read in Turkey. In the poem, a lonely young widow, "the Lady Amine, mother of Muhammed," brings into the world the "bearer of brilliant light" in a radiance that illuminates the entire Arabian peninsula. The infant looks toward heaven and speaks: "My people, alas my people," and the whole world, down to its smallest particle, recites:

> *"Welcome, O healer of our wounds.*
> *Welcome, O refuge of erring nations.*
> *Welcome, O helper of the helpless.*
> *Welcome, O thou who holdest the hand of the fallen."*

At the same time, the angels in heaven and the future generations of Moslems intone the "Salutation to the Prophet" (Selat-un-Nebi), which Turkish congregations still repeat to this day: "God bless our Lord Muhammed, the Apostle of the untaught."

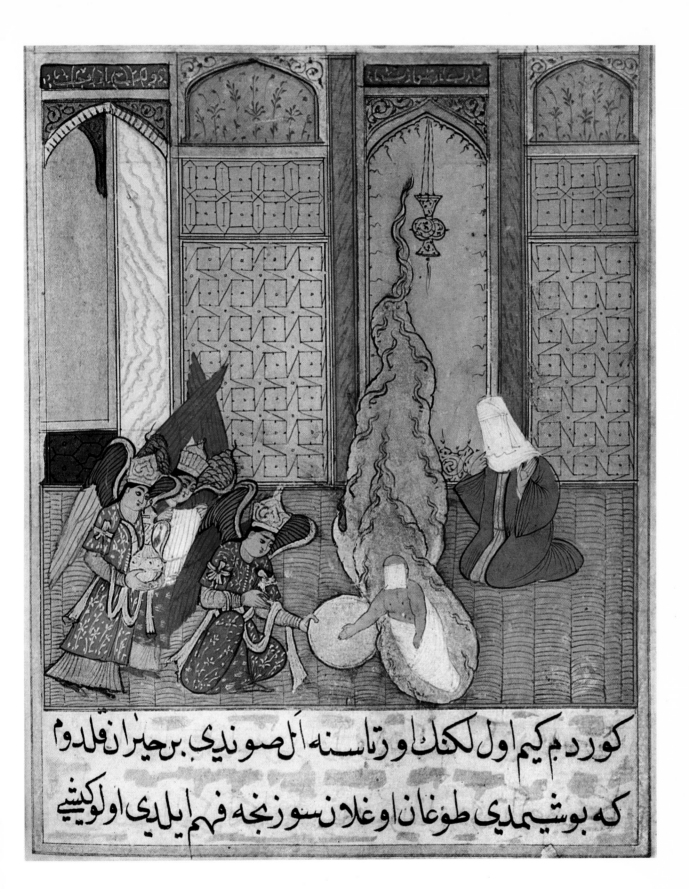

کوردم کیم اول لکنك ورتاسنه الصوندی برحیزان قلدوم
که بوشیمدی طوغان اوغلان سوزنخه فهم ایلدی اولوکینی

PLATE FIVE

Muhammed on Mount Hira

From the three-volume manuscript, Siyer-un-Nebi (Progress of the Prophet): a copy, executed in 1594 by Ahmet Nur b. Mustafa for Murad III, of an earlier manuscript dated 1368, whose author was Mustafa b. Yusuf b. Omer Erzeni Dariri. One of 125 miniatures. 16th century. 15×14.5 cm. Courtesy of the Topkapu Museum (H. 1221–23), Istanbul.

IBNIHISHAM,[10] one of the Prophet's first biographers, gives us the following account of the beginning of Muhammed's religious mission:

"When Muhammed, the Apostle of God, reached the age of forty, God manifested through him His compassion for the universe and the glad tidings thereof to mankind. . . . God made him love solitude. . . . He would journey until there were no houses. . . . And not a stone or a tree that he passed by but would speak to him: 'Peace upon thee, O Apostle of God.' And the Apostle would turn around to the right and to the left and look behind, seeing nothing except trees and stones. . . . In the month of Ramadan, the Apostle of God went to (Mount) Hira. . . . When came the night on which God Almighty, in His mercy, granted him prophethood, Gabriel came to him with the command of God. 'Gabriel came to me,' said the Apostle of God, with a written scroll, while I was asleep, and said: "Read." I said: "I cannot read." . . . He pressed me with it until I thought it was death. . . . And he said: "Read, in the name of thy Lord, Who created man." . . . And he departed. . . . And I awoke. . . . And it was as if the scripture were written on my heart. . . . And I went until I was midway on the mountain and heard a sound from heaven saying: "O Muhammed, thou art the Apostle of God, and I am Gabriel." I raised my head to heaven and saw him. . . . And I stood staring at him and could move neither forward nor backward. Then I turned my face away from him to the horizon, but toward whatever region of the sky I looked, I saw him as before.' "

The painter has chosen the moment when "midway on the mountain" Muhammed sees the awe-inspiring vision of the angel. The effect of transfiguration of the material landscape into the spiritual "horizon of truth" of the Koran is achieved by the exclusive use of gold leaf. Contours are indicated in burnt sienna, while a few touches of white and green help to give volume and to moderate an exaggerated effect of warmth in color.

The Arabian desert landscape is depicted with elements of the Central Asian steppe. The steep hills that Muhammed faces are in the tall conical shapes preferred by the pre-Islamic painters of Turkestan (Ill. 10). The shrublike trees, characteristic of desert climates, emulate the patterns of Turkestani models of the 7th and 8th centuries but with a new and solemn feeling, as if they were still secretly addressing Muhammed. In "the highest part of the horizon," as the Koran describes it, where Muhammed first saw the angel, a few white clouds in Central Asian style have been placed.

Muhammed himself is an ethereally white figure standing on a slightly oblique axis, as if thrown backwards and falling down in terror before the vision. The Prophet's hands are raised in a gesture of awe that is already the first movement in the ritual Moslem prayer: the *tekbir* or "glorification of God."

طاغنه چقدی طاغك یاروسنه ایرشبجك ینه رسول حضرتك
قولاغنه اولکدن فاتی برهیبتلو آواز کلدی آی این نرید یا محمد

Muhammed Praying with Khadija and Ali

From the three-volume manuscript, Siyer-un-Nebi *(Progress of the Prophet): a copy, executed in 1594 by Ahmet Nur b. Mustafa for Murad III, of an earlier manuscript dated 1364, whose author was Mustafa b. Yusuf b. Omer Erzeni Dariri. One of 125 miniatures. 16th century. 15 × 14.5 cm. Courtesy of the Topkapu Museum (H. 1221–23), Istanbul.*

IN THIS miniature we see a representation of the beginning of the Islamic prayer ritual. In Plate V the Prophet of Islam is shown on Mount Hira receiving the first verses of the Koranic revelation. Awed by the sight of the archangel, Muhammed fled from the mountain to his house in Mecca and confided to his wife Khadija his fears of losing his reason. As related by the 8th-century Arab historian, Ibni Hisham, the narrative continues:

"Khadija said: 'Rejoice, O Muhammed, and persevere. . . . Verily, I hope that thou wilt be the prophet of this people.' . . . And she was the first to believe in God and in His Apostle. . . . Through her, God lightened the burden of His Prophet. He never heard things abhorrent to him, which contradicted him and imputed falsehood to him and grieved him, but that God comforted him through her when he returned home. She strengthened him, lightened his burden, confirmed him, and made his mission easier. May God have mercy upon her. . . . Then revelation to the Apostle of God ceased . . . so that he was distressed, and he despaired. Then Gabriel came to him with the *Surat of the Morning*. . . . The Almighty said: 'By the morning and the night when darkness falls, thy Lord hath not forsaken nor hated thee.' . . . Prayer was prescribed upon the Apostle . . . and so he prayed. . . . And the Apostle of God came to Khadija . . . and he performed the ritual prayer for her as Gabriel had done for him, and she prayed with him."[11]

The Prophet stands in the center of this scene, leading the prayer while Khadija and the ten-year-old child Ali, cousin of Muhammed, take part. All three are at the stage of the prayer where the supplicant stands with his hands folded as if tied. This gesture indicates complete submission to God. In the manner of pre-Islamic Central Asian holy figures, the Prophet is entirely surrounded by a nimbus of light. He wears an immaculate turban, and his coat is green, the color symbolizing the Koranic revelation. The dark lining of the coat is an allusion to the mystic significance of the Koran.

Khadija, standing behind in feminine modesty, wears blue, the shade of purity and restraint. Her garment is lined with another hue: the red of love. She also has a flaming halo of holiness, but only around her head. Ali has no halo but wears the traditional green turban of Islamic teachers. His dark coat foretells that he is to be one of the initiators of the mystic interpretation of the Koran.

Through the windows can be seen the gardens of paradise in the Spring of Islam. Behind a ruby arcade supported by green columns, the celestial trees are blooming against a golden sky. The pink bloom is the peach, symbolizing the beginning of divine love, while the white bloom of the almond tree is a reference to the essential and kernel-like qualities of the Koranic revelation. One of the rivers of paradise is seen flowing downwards, representing a torrent of mercy.

The room is covered with allegoric patterns. Islamic mysticism interprets the star mentioned in the Koran as the knowledge of God in the soul. Thus the varied shapes of stars on the mauve wall under the windows and on the rose carpet are the souls of believers. The cyclamen carpet offers a flower pattern with a starry effect. The crossed swords on the closed panel of a blue shutter represent another allegorical pattern: *Seyfullah,* the Sword of God, wounding the human heart with divine love.

قیود زا ایجره وکردی کوردیکم رسول حضرتی خدیجه خانون برله
نماز قلور لر خدیجه خانون رسول اللهٔ صول یاننده دورپدور

The Death of Muhammed

From the three-volume manuscript, Siyer-un-Nebi *(Progress of the Prophet): a copy, executed in 1594 by Ahmet Nur b. Mustafa for Murad III, of an earlier manuscript dated 1368, whose author was Mustafa b. Yusuf b. Omer Erzeni Dariri. One of 125 miniatures. 16th century. 15 × 14.5 cm. Courtesy of the Topkapu Museum (H. 1221–23), Istanbul.*

WHEN MUHAMMED reached the age of sixty-three, the Islamic religion appeared to be consolidated. The Prophet of Islam hinted more than once at his approaching term, although few understood the meaning of his words. During his fatal illness, Muhammed tried to attend the mosque and appealed to the Moslems to preserve Islamic faith and brotherly love. Notwithstanding his forewarnings, when he died in 632 uttering the words "Nay, let me go back to the Exalted Comforter," his death seemed to the Moslem community an incredible catastrophe.

Muhammed lies horizontally in the center of the miniature, already covered with the "few yards of cloth" with which, according to the 13th-century poet Yunus Emre, the material world hid and buried the spiritual message of the Prophet. He is shown on a bed that is placed in the Turkish manner on the straw matting of the room. He was to be buried in the humble hut in which he died.

Leaning over the Prophet's veiled face is his friend Abubekr, who succeeded him as head of the Islamic community. Abubekr is reported to have kissed him and gone out to the dumbfounded people waiting outside, whom he thus addressed: "Oh people, if you worship Muhammed, Muhammed is dead. If you worship God, God is living and immortal."

Fatima, the daughter of the Prophet, is shown standing in a dark red robe whose color symbolizes a bleeding heart. Her head is surrounded with a halo. Fatima, who was to write an elegy for her father and soon thereafter to die of grief for him, wipes her tears away with a handkerchief while, with her other hand she indicates the dead Prophet.

In the background is shown Ali, the husband of Fatima, mourning over his lost friend. The two children of Ali and Fatima, the future martyrs Hasan and Husein, kneel in the foreground, the one weeping and the other pounding his face in grief. Like Muhammed, whom he resembled, the one wears a green coat; the other, who resembled Ali, is clothed in the same deep shade of blue. Both wear flaming halos.

The walls of the room are divided in Turkish style into panels of different hues, in this case violet, blue, and purple. A design of swords and arrows framed in stars and other geometric shapes covers the walls and appears to try to express, in the confusion and irregularity of its lines, the piercing sorrow of those whom death has separated from Muhammed. On the windowpanes are patterns suggesting tears. An echo of the feelings of those who survived has come down to us in a line from a poem by another of Muhammed's friends, Hassan b. Thabet: "O best of men that ever walked the earth, leave us not!"

With this last illustration from the *Siyer-un-Nebi,* it is appropriate to give some information on the author of the book. Mustafa Erzeni was born in the 14th century in the eastern Turkish city of Erzurum. Although blind from birth, he traveled as far as Egypt, where the Mameluk sultan Berkuk asked him to translate "into our Turkish language" the classical Arabic works on the life of Muhammed. Sheyh Ejmeluddin, a contemporary whom Erzeni consulted, encouraged him. Both men felt the importance of the enterprise, the blindness of Erzeni seeming to them an allegory of the spiritual blindness of mankind. As Erzeni knelt before him to receive his blessing, Ejmeluddin advised him to write a commentary on Abu Hasan-el-Bekri's life of Muhammed rather than on Ibni Hisham's work. After some hesitation, Erzeni combined the two works, adding to his book many mystical and popular poems and interpretations originating in his native land.

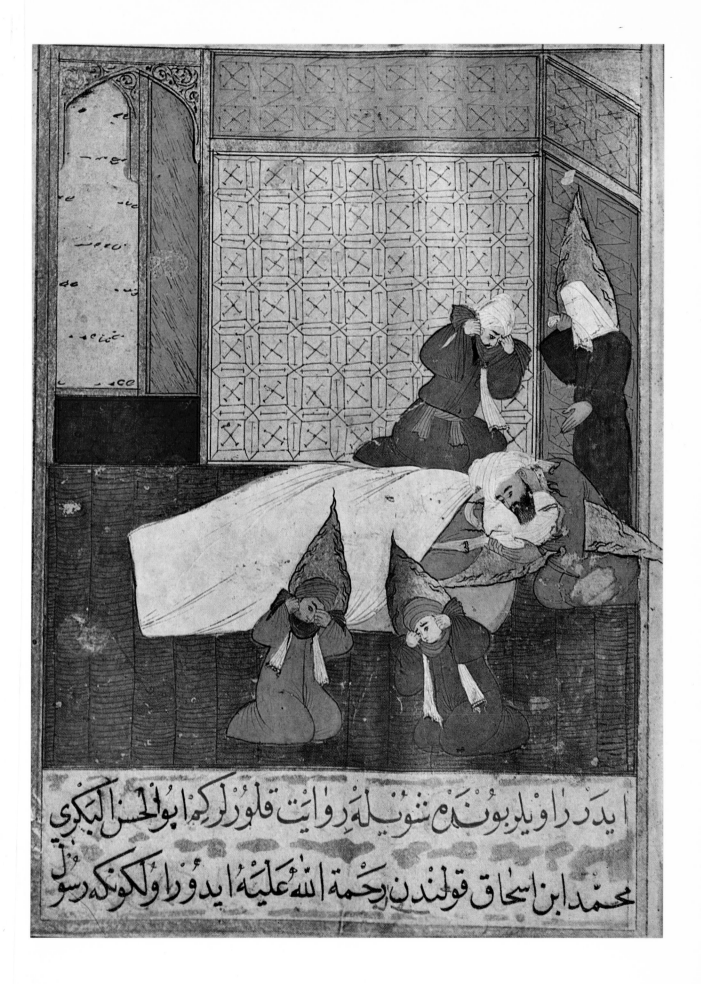

اى دردا اولو بونڭ غم شو نیله روایت قلورلرکم ابوالحسن البکری

محمد ابن اسحاق قولندن رحمة الله علیه اید دردا اولو رکه دسول

The Enthronement of Selim II

From the Nüzheti-Esrar el-Ehbar der Seferi Sigetvar *(Account of Secret Events during the Campaign of Sigeth), dated 1568 and written by Ahmed Feridun Pasha, with a dedication to the grand vizier Sokullu Mehmed Pasha. 16th century. 29×41 cm. Courtesy of the Topkapu Museum (H. 1339), Istanbul.*

THIS LARGE and colorful composition covers two pages of the manuscript in which it appears. The implications of the scene demand some explanation. In 1566, Sultan Süleyman, called "the Magnificent" in Europe and "the Legislator" in Turkey, died at the age of seventy-four from the strains of a military campaign in Hungary. His death was concealed until his successor could be summoned. The victorious army marched homeward, unaware that in the state carriage which they escorted lay the dead sultan. One night the army was awakened by the sound of hundreds of voices reciting the Koranic verse: "All is mortal except the countenance of thy Lord, full of glory and generosity," whereupon they understood that the sultan was dead. His heir, Selim, after a hurried sword-girding ceremony in Istanbul, rushed to Belgrade—then a Turkish city—to await the army. He greeted them at dawn, arrayed in mourning garb, his palms open toward heaven to beg for God's mercy upon his father Süleyman, whose coffin was advancing among funerary torches. The hills surrounding Belgrade, which we see outlined in blue against a rosy sky in the miniature, echoed with the army's prayer for the dead.

Selim retired later to a cupola-shaped imperial tent—a symbol of sovereignty in Central Asian tradition—to receive the homage of the army, and it is here that we see him sitting under the folds of red and purple hangings decorated with giant patterns of golden leaves. Two other canopies, slanted at different angles, insure compositional unity between the two parts of the picture. The blue and the lilac skies of the two canopies carry flights of legendary birds, the *humay* and the long-necked *anka,* which are both symbols of the "rulers of the world, the Kaans of Turan and Iran." The sultan's imposing turban is decorated with a feather said to have been detached from the mythical phoenix, Devlet Kushu. Selim, called "the Fair," is portrayed with a blond beard and is larger than the other figures. He wears ermine and a sleeveless blue coat.

The son of Sultan Süleyman and the beautiful Roxelane sits uneasily on the golden throne of his father. Süleyman had been one of a long line of rulers, intrepid on the battlefield and devoted to the service of the people. Selim II, a poet and a musician, a lover of wine and women, was not considered worthy to reign. While the army outside shouts its disapproval of the new sultan, we see the dignitaries of the empire aligned, their hands folded in a gesture of submission. They wear very large turbans in the rounded form of the period. Their coats of Turkish brocades and velvets are in various hues of red, blue, violet, and black, according to their court functions, and show the traditional large patterns of stars, crescents, tulips, leaves, the Buddhist jewel design of ancient Turkestan, and the like. The faces are typically Turkish in aspect, several of them being actual portraits. The stalwart grand vizier, Sokullu Mehmed Pasha, can be seen standing on the right side of the sultan together with Selim's tutor, his master of ceremonies, and his groom. On the sultan's left are his sword- and seal-bearers. Janissary officers, represented in smaller size than the viziers, advance across the foreground, wearing on their headgear the insignia of their rank. Some have rebellious expressions as they prepare to bow and kneel down on the pink carpet before the throne, where they must kiss the fringe of a scarf at the Sultan's feet in a traditional gesture of homage. One officer wears the green coat of an army judge. The miniaturist has succeeded remarkably well in capturing the irony that underlies the grandeur of the scene.

PLATE NINE

The Turkish Army Departing for the Caucasian Campaign, April 1578

From the Nusretname-i Aali *(Aali's Book of Victory), written in 1584 in Turkish by the historian Aali. 16th century. Two miniatures, 18 × 30 cm each. Courtesy of the Topkapu Museum (H. 1365), Istanbul.*

AGAINST a golden sky we see the slopes of blue hills and a mauve field filled with a multitude of figures in a crowded composition which has yet been able to achieve a dynamic unity through a single direction of movement. The Turkish army in campaign array was a sight which the people of Istanbul saw whenever danger arose at one of the remote borders of the Ottoman Empire. The army consisted of two forces: the regulars stationed in the capital city and the reserves supplied by the provinces. The commander-in-chief rode in a procession which carried flags and the relics of the Prophet. His retinue sometimes included historians and painters to recount the events of the campaign, and it is to the historian Aali, who accompanied the army, that we owe the text of the *Nusretname*. The splendor of the scene was enhanced by a military band that played epic tunes on Central Asian instruments as it advanced in a traditional step. Galleys manned by the Algerian and Tunisian sea forces of the Ottoman Empire transported the army over the Bosporus while the detonation of guns from military castles and lighthouses saluted the outgoing expedition. According to Central Asian tradition, a ceremonial tent was pitched outside the walls of the city in the vicinity of a country mosque such as the one we see at the top left-hand corner of the scene, and here a religious service was attended.

In the left center of the picture we see the commander-in-chief, Lala Mustafa Pasha, represented larger than the other figures and recognizably portrayed. Wearing a red costume, a maroon jacket, and a golden scabbard, he rides a white horse caparisoned in gold and is followed by two pages. Behind him advance contingents of the sultan's cavalry mounted on graceful and brilliantly colored horses that may have been sired by the "heavenly steeds" described by the Chinese as the horses of the ancient nomads. Some of the riders are dressed in ordinary 16th-century Turkish clothes. The lancers wear costumes and helmets that have not changed greatly from those of the warriors depicted in 8th-century Turkestani paintings and sculpture (Ill. 7). The army carries banners and horsetails mounted on poles, as did ancient Central Asian armies.

The commander-in-chief is preceded by the infantry corps of the Janissaries, whose officers, wearing badges, are represented in larger size than the soldiers. The Janissaries' elongated felt cap is said to evoke the memory of the sleeve of their patron saint, Haci Bektash, as he extended his arm over their heads to bless the corps. Two *solak* guards may be recognized by their aprons.

The right wing of the army was usually reserved to the Anatolian forces, and these we see in the miniature caracoling with their pennants on the blue hills. At the top right is a group of three governors of Anatolian provinces that bordered the troubled area, the Caucasian frontier. In the left wing of the army march contingents from the European provinces of the empire. (Lala Mustafa's European soldiers were the Tartars of Crimea.) Members of the engineering corps carry axes attached to their belts.

Still remote from this brilliant scene are the hardships of campaigning, the charge to the deafening sound of drums and trumpets, and the thunderous voice with which the soldiers, when confronting death, proclaim in Turkish army tradition: "Allahu Ekber (God is the Highest)!"

Episode from the Festivities at Istanbul in September 1720

From the two-volume Surname-i Vehbi *(Vehbi's Account of Festivities), written in Turkish by the poet Vehbi and illustrated with 137 miniatures by Levni. 18th century. Two pages, 36×23 cm each. Courtesy of the Topkapu Museum (A. III 3594), Istanbul.*

BETWEEN 1720 and 1722, Istanbul was the scene of a number of popular festivities organized to celebrate the weddings of the daughters of Ahmed III and the circumcision and entrance into school of his sons. These congratulatory entertainments were recorded by Levni in a series of colorful miniatures.

The 18th century is called in Turkish history the "period of tulips." The sudden popularity of this flower, which had come from Central Asia seven centuries before, symbolized the mood of the time. The citizens of Istanbul had finally renounced the austere traditions of the Moslem Middle Ages, and pleasure became the order of the day. Instead of the great mosques of the past, palaces, kiosks, gardens, and fountains were built. The painter Levni and the great lyric poet Nedim dedicated their best talents to the portrayal of entertainment. The law finally had to intervene to check the luxury of flower gardens, the size of ladies' headgear, and the width of their ribbons.

The festive events of the imperial family and those of the people were celebrated together in ceremonies that sometimes lasted for weeks. Giant feasts were prepared in the palace kitchens, and presents were exchanged between the sultan and the professional corporations. The latter organized parades led by masters of ceremonies who carried jingling batons. Decorated chariots, effigies of legendary or exotic figures, emblems of various crafts, and representations of historical events filed past the sultan.

Levni, like other 18th-century painters, prefers softer colors and makes little use of gold illumination. The love of movement, the powers of observation, and the inclination toward humorous interpretation that we see in this miniature are characteristic of all Turkish painting.

Against a background of yellow earth and azure sky a procession moves along curving lines toward the sultan, who sits at the upper right corner, the place of honor. The imperial kiosk is surmounted by a curved roof in the shape of a ceremonial tent. The sultan wears a brown robe, a lilac fur-lined jacket, and a turban in the fashion of the 17th and 18th centuries. He is attended by a child prince in red and by two chamberlains, all of whom fold their hands in respect. A cloth with embroidered panels secludes the court assembly from the public. Janissaries guard the rear of the tent. Attendants of the imperial household, dressed in the various colors of their functions, advance toward the exterior, preceded by a clerical person in dark green and a figure in deep red wearing a golden belt and a conical hat. Two blue-clad treasurers in tall turbans are seen receiving the proffered gifts. A green-and-fawn tent shelters the grand vizier Ibrahim Pasha, husband of the sultan's talented daughter Fatima. He sits on a red mattress, reclining against a blue cushion. In a third tent stand three figures who, according to their garb, are two viziers and a professor.

The procession advances from the top left of the composition, where an ambulant bath attendant, in a carriage decorated with towels, is busy washing a client's hair. A group holding presents is surrounded by soldiers carrying rifles and preceded by musicians. The line of the procession curves inward at the level of a raised platform where there are some white objects that might be tapers, fuses, fireworks, or sweets. At the bottom left, following a group of armed men, is the corporation of the jesters, including clowns and acrobats with the implements of their gay trade. At the lower right, the candlemakers are presenting their gift, and two gold-crowned palace attendants carry bags of gold coins to be strewn over the crowd.

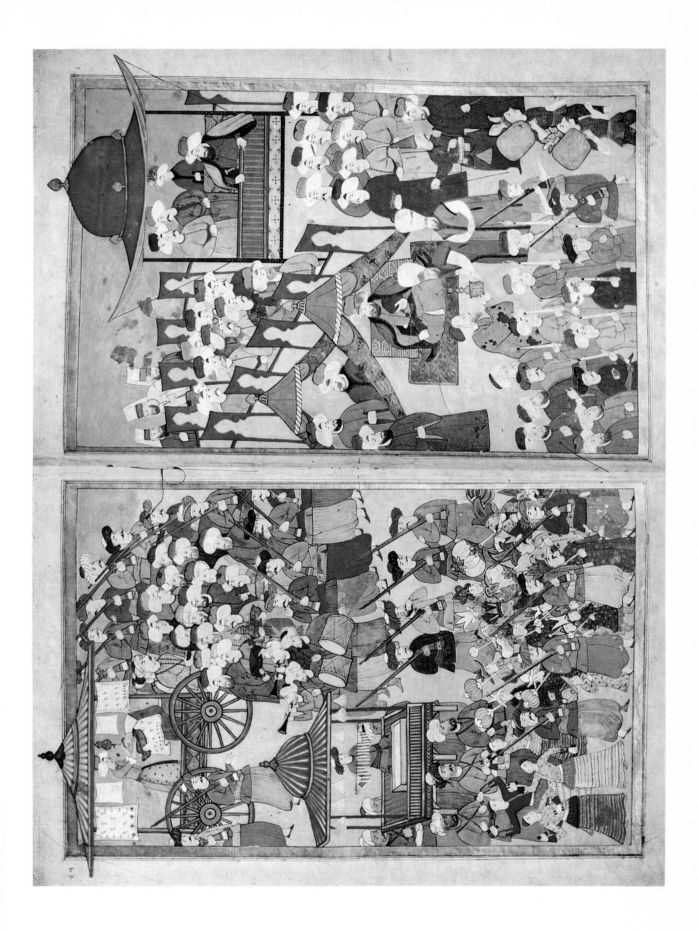

PLATE ELEVEN

Nocturnal Party on the Sea of Marmora in September 1720

From the two-volume Surname-i Vehbi *(Vehbi's Account of Festivities), written in Turkish by the poet Vehbi and illustrated with 137 miniatures by Levni. 18th century. Two pages, 36×23 cm each. Courtesy of the Topkapu Museum (A. III 3594), Istanbul.*

THIS NIGHT scene in the sea-girt city of Istanbul is painted in several cool nuances of blue and mauve, while silver illumination is used for the surface of the sea. Red details seem to glow against the nocturnal blue. The composition is a descriptive one, the two-page spread being covered with figures grouped along horizontal lines to suggest the peaceful mood of the night.

The subject is a continuation of the one depicted in Plate X. Night has not put an end to the festivities. An acrobatic entertainment is staged on the sea near the foot of the sultan's palace. Between a galley and a galleon anchored there and a tree on the shore, ropes have been stretched to form a half-marine and half-aerial stage. On the pairs of ropes stretched horizontally between the two ships, we see advancing—probably moved by wires—a red carriage drawn by a puppet horse ridden by a puppet groom. Other puppets dressed in the town costume of Istanbul ladies and transparently veiled in white, as was then the custom, have been placed in the carriage and are looking with curiosity out of the window. On the water, three dancers, perched precariously on small floating rafts, are clicking their castanets and whirling to the strains of *kocekce* tunes played by musicians in boats. These, according to custom, are young boys dressed in feminine garb to replace women, who did not generally perform in public. The drums, clarinets, tambourines, and kettledrums that we see being so lustily played by the turbaned musicians in the two boats, are instruments represented in early Central Asian painting and sculpture as, for example, in the 2nd-century Tirmiz frieze in Turkestan.

At the top right, outlined against the deep blue sky, stands the Pearl Kiosk, its walls rising from the seashore. We may imagine that behind these high walls, under the cypresses, the tulip gardens were illuminated with colored glass lanterns in whose glow the flowers seemed to be aflame. From a little kiosk built directly on the water in the Turkish manner, the Sultan watches the entertainment. Sitting on a low sofa and reclining against a golden pillow, he wears a pink robe and an orange pelisse. Seated or standing respectfully around him and all wearing fur-lined coats, are several young princes, an African dignitary in a cherry coat (probably the chief eunuch), and a chamberlain in purple. Looking into the kiosk above the lattice-work screens, we can see that the interior is decorated with blue tiles.

At the top left of the picture, a stately galleon, entirely painted with decorative designs and national emblems, is filled with the dignitaries of the empire. This state galleon is much larger than the other vessels and is adorned with a red standard strewn with golden stars and moons: symbols of brilliance. In the foreground, settled in their graceful *kayiks* or rowboats and wearing topcoats against the chilliness of the night, the people of Istanbul watch and seem to discuss the wonders the of water festival.

28

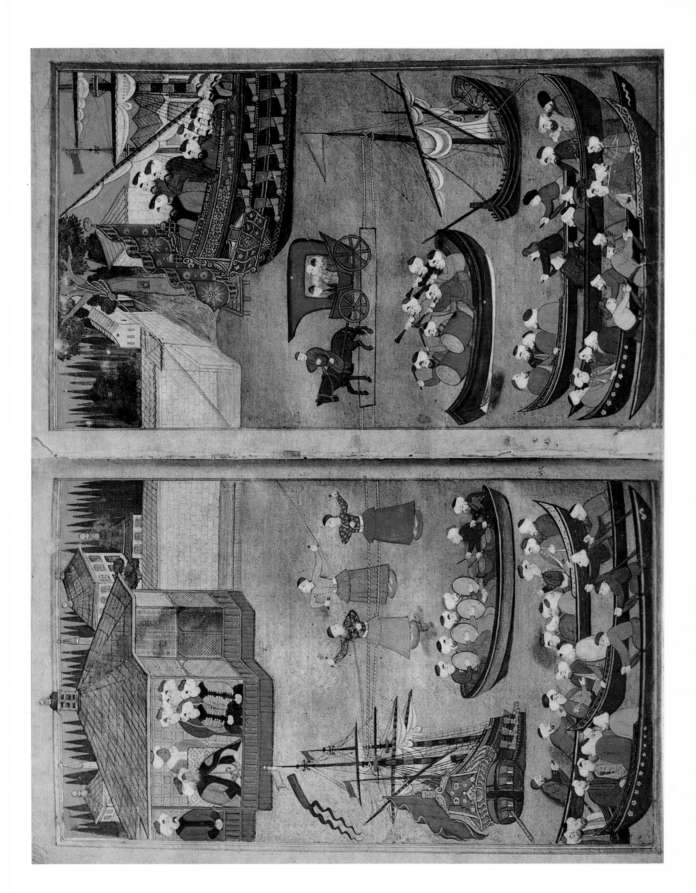

PLATE TWELVE

A Turkish Lady of the 18th Century

A miniature by Levni. 18th century. 17×9.5 cm. Courtesy of the Topkapu Museum, Istanbul.

WOMEN, who are not generally represented taking part in public gatherings, are a favorite subject in interior scenes by Turkish miniaturists. The conventional appearance which Turkish painting and poetry have given to women is related to the representations of feminine deities in pre-Islamic Turkestani art. A beautiful woman's face is compared to the shining moon, and she is called a "moon-faced Khotan image" or a *bud,* which means an idol to be worshipped. The ideal of physical beauty remains almost unchanged from the days of the 8th-century sculptures and paintings of east Turkestan down to the 18th century. The rounded oval face, the low forehead, and the Hunnic cut of the eye were the hieratically fixed features of the type that Persian literature has also celebrated under the name of "Turkish beauty." The costumes and headdresses have changed very little in the course of the centuries, as one may observe by comparing figures in the 8th-century fresco at Bezeklik in Turkestan with a 17th-century Turkish miniature (Ills. 11 and 12). When Levni's heroine, in the privacy of her home, discards her veil, she appears wearing over her intricately braided hair an elaborately decorated headdress similar to one shown in a clay sculpture of a thousand years earlier in Shortchuk. From the time of the 7th-century murals in Panj-Kent down to our days, Turkish women have always braided their hair in numerous tresses.

Levni has painted a lady in pink, in a reclining position, resting her head on a blue-and-gold pillow as she leans on one elbow. The colors are soft, the lines gracefully naturalistic. The lady's eyes are closed, either in sleep or in daydreaming. Her appearance follows the description of beauty given by the Ottoman court poets: her slim body seems to be swaying like a cypress, and her face is pale like the moon. The closely knit brows and the haughty posture of the head indicate a "cruel charmer." Levni seems to compare the lady to a carnation. Her pink coat has a carnation pattern, and one of the golden carnations in the foreground enfolds the painter's signature, perhaps as a sign of homage to the model. Under the short-sleeved pink coat the lady wears a long-sleeved green robe and a white gauze blouse. She has unclasped her golden belt, and her bosom is half bare, similar to the décolleté of the 8th-century Shortchuk figure whose headdress hers resembles. Her bare feet emerge from violet trousers, and her toenails, like her fingernails, appear to be dyed with henna. The lady wears golden jewelry.

This miniature is one of a series of over fifty plates, most of them portraits, representing Ahmed III and the ladies, musicians, pages, and other members of his court. The painter Levni is said to have been born in Edirne and to have entered the Nakishane or Academy of Painting at the Topkapu Palace when he was young. He became chief painter of the court during the reign of Mustafa II and probably held the same post under Ahmed III. He died in 1732 and was buried at Ayvanseray in Istanbul.

NOTES

1. R. Grousset: *L'Empire des Steppes*, Paris, 1948, pp. 37 and 55. See also Plates XXV and XCVI in S. J. Rudenko: *Culture of the Altai Mountains in the Scythian Period* (in Russian), Moscow, 1953.

2. Rudenko, *op. cit.*, Plate LXXXIX.

3. E. Diez: *Die Kunst der Islamischen Völker*, Berlin, 1915, p. 186.

4. Professor Z. V. Togan of Istanbul University is preparing this manuscript for publication.

5. A. Y. Yakubovsky: *Altin Ordu ve Inhitati* (Turkish translation by H. Eren), Istanbul, 1955, p. 142.

6. Academy Nauk, *Paintings of Ancient Panj-Kent*, Moscow, 1954, Plate XXII.

7. H. Härtel: *Turfan und Gandhara*, Berlin, 1957, p. 19 and Ill. 20.

8. V. Minorsky: *The Chester Beatty Library: A Catalogue of Turkish Manuscripts and Miniatures*, Dublin, 1958, p. 21.

9. Other copies of the *Siyer-un-Nebi* are in the Türk-Islam Eserleri Museum in Istanbul, in the Chester Beatty Collection in Dublin, and in the Dresden Library.

10. Ibni Hisham: *Al-Siret-un-Nabaviyya* (in Arabic), Cairo, 1936, pp. 252–255.

11. *Ibid.* pp. 257–261.

SELECTED BIBLIOGRAPHY

N. Bayrakdar: *Catalogue of Illustrated Turkish Manuscripts in the Süleymaniye Library* (in Turkish), Istanbul (in preparation)

K. Cig: *Illustrated Turkish Manuscripts in the Türk-Islam Eserleri Museum* (in Turkish), Istanbul, 1959

——: *Catalogue of Illustrated Turkish Manuscripts in the Topkapu Museum* (in Turkish), Istanbul (in preparation)

E. Diez and O. Aslanapa: *Turkish Art* (in Turkish), Istanbul, 1955

H. Edhem: *Tagebuch der Aegyptischen Expedition des Sultans Selim I*, Weimar, 1916

E. Esin: *Journey to Turkestan* (in Turkish), Ankara, 1959

M. Ipsiroglu and S. Eyuboglu: *Sur l'Album du Conquérant*, Istanbul, 1954

M. Kashgari: *Mitteltürkischer Wortschatz nach Mahmud-el-Kashgari* (German translation by C. Brockelmann), Leipzig, 1928

S. Kisilev: *Ancient History of Southern Siberia* (in Russian), Moscow, 1951

R. Melul: *Documents on the History of Turkish Miniature Painting* (in Turkish), Istanbul, 1933

V. Minorsky: *The Chester Beatty Library: A Catalogue of Turkish Manuscripts and Miniatures*, Dublin, 1958

A. P. Okladinov: *The Ancient Population of Siberia and its Cultures*, Russian Translation Series, Vol. I, No. 1, Peabody Museum of Archeology and Ethnology, Harvard University, Cambridge, Massachusetts, 1959

T. Öz: *Works of Art from the Collection of Mehmed II at the Topkapu Museum* (in Turkish), Ankara, 1950

E. Schroeder: "Ahmed Musa and Shams al-Din, a Review of Fourteenth Century Painting," *Ars Islamica*, Vol. VI, No. 2, Ann Arbor, 1939

I. Skoutchine and H. Edem: *Les manuscrits orientaux de la Bibliothèque de l'Université d'Istanbul*, Paris, 1933

S. Ünver: *The Painter Nigari* (in Turkish), Ankara, 1946

——: *The Painter Nakshi* (in Turkish), Istanbul, 1949

——: *Levni* (in English), Istanbul, 1951

A. von Le Coq: *Buddhistische Spätantike in Mittelasien*, Berlin, 1923–33.

——: *Chotscho*, Berlin, 1913

ILL. 1. Fabulous beast from felt-appliqué tent cover. Pazyryk, Altai. 4th century B.C. Ermitage Museum, Leningrad.

ILL. 2. Head of a Hunnic type, sculptured in terra cotta. Khotan, Turkestan. 3rd century(?). A. Stein: *Ancient Khotan,* London, 1907, Plate XLV.

ILL. 3. Popular type of Turkish leather marionette. Contemporary. S. E. Siyavushgil: *Karagöz,* Ankara, 1955, last plate (unnumbered).

ILL. 5. Posture common in ancient Turkestan. Fragment of a mural. Panj-Kent, Turkestan. 7th century. Academy Nauk, *Paintings of Ancient Panj-Kent,* Moscow, 1954, Plate X.

ILL. 6. Crowned figures of ancient Turkestan. Mural. Panj-Kent, Turkestan. 7th century. Academy Nauk, *Paintings of Ancient Panj-Kent,* Moscow, 1954, Plate XVI.

ILL. 4. Posture common in Turkish art. Fragment of an undated miniature. Courtesy of Topkapu Museum, Istanbul.

ILL. 7. Clay sculpture of warrior wearing a pointed helmet. Shortchuk, Turkestan. 8th century. A. von Le Coq: *Bilderatlas zur Kunst und Kulturgeschichte Mittelasiens,* Berlin, 1925, p. 59, Ill. 67.

ILL. 8. Fragment of clay sculpture showing flaming halo characteristic of Central Asian art. Tun-huang, Kansu. Before 11th century. P. Pelliot: *Les Grottes de Touen-Houang,* Paris, 1920, Plate CCCLXXIV.

ILL. 9. Felt appliqué representing a nomad goddess wearing a crown-shaped headgear. Pazyryk, Altai. 4th century B.C. S. J. Rudenko: *Culture of the Altaic Mountains in the Scythian Period,* Moscow, 1953, Plate XCV.

ILL. 10. Detail of mountains in ancient Turkestani mural. Bezeklik, Turkestan. 9th century. Courtesy of Museum für Völkerkunde, Berlin.

ILL. 11. Detail from ancient Turkestani mural showing a lady wearing a headgear with feathers. Bezeklik, Turkestan. 8th century. Courtesy of Museum für Völkerkunde, Berlin.

ILL. 12. Detail from Turkish miniature showing a lady wearing a conical bridal headgear with feathers. 17th century. Courtesy of Topkapu Museum, Istanbul.